Trumpet Artistry
Classical Solos for Trumpet & Piano

Alfred Lang, *Trumpet*

Harriet Wingreen, *Piano*

To access audio visit:
www.halleonard.com/mylibrary

Enter Code
3655-0071-9025-2080

ISBN 978-1-59615-227-4

EXCLUSIVELY DISTRIBUTED BY

HAL•LEONARD®

Visit Hal Leonard Online at
www.halleonard.com

Contact Us:
Hal Leonard
7777 West Bluemound Road
Milwaukee, WI 53213
Email: info@halleonard.com

In Europe contact:
Hal Leonard Europe Limited
42 Wigmore Street
Marylebone, London, W1U 2RN
Email: info@halleonardeurope.com

In Australia contact:
Hal Leonard Australia Pty. Ltd.
4 Lentara Court
Cheltenham, Victoria, 3192 Australia
Email: info@halleonard.com.au

Trumpet Artistry

Classical Solos for Trumpet & Piano

All selections edited by Alfred Lang

FOREWORD

When I was first approached to record this music, I did not give any thought to how hard it would be to lay trumpet parts down on pre-existing piano tracks. It soon become apparent, however, that this is no easy task. Rubatos, accelerandos, and fermatas are all much easier to execute when communicating with a live accompanist. But then I realized – what I was going through is EXACTLY what you, the end user of this book, go through every time you play along with the accompaniment tracks. I had just encountered the true Music Minus One experience! So, a word of advice: don't worry about catching downbeats exactly right or being "in sync" with the piano every measure. It is more important to make beautiful music.

Most of the music is straight ahead, but I have included a few comments regarding two of the pieces.

Allegro Spiritoso – Jean Baptiste Senaille

I found it necessary to double-tongue much of this piece. If you have problems, try adding slurs in appropriate spots. Running sixteenth notes can be played slur two/tongue two. Experiment. Nothing says you must adhere to the articulations indicated; particularly when the piece was not originally written for the trumpet.

Sonata Movements – William de Fesch

The A-flat/B-flat trill on the last beat of measure 6 in the opening *Largo* should be fingered thusly: 2-3 for the A-flat and 1-2-3 for the B-flat.

All selections were played on a medium-large bore, B-flat Bach Stradivarius, Model 37, serial number 39682.

-Alfred Lang
Silverado, California

En fermant les yeux

from "Manon"

Jules Massenet
(1842-1912)

Allegro Spiritoso

Jean Babtiste Senaillé
(1687-1730)

4 taps (2 measures) precede music

Lively ♩ = 138

Cantique de Noël

Adolphe-Charles Adam
(1803-1856)

Air

from Suite No.3

Johann Sebastian Bach
(1685-1750)

Allegro

Franz Schubert
(1797-1828)

Concert Rondo

Wolfgang Amadeus Mozart
(1756-1791)

4 taps (1 measure) precede music

Allegro

12

Little Adagio
from "L'Arlesienne"

Georges Bizet
(1838-1875)

Adagio

Le Tambourin

Jean Philippe Rameau
(1683-1764)

3 taps (1 1/2 meas.) precede music

Allegro molto

Sonata Movements
from Flute Sonata in D Major

George Friedrich Handel
(1685-1759)

8 taps (1 measure) precede music

Adagio (in 8)

3 taps (1 measure) precede music

Menuet

18

Allegro

Theme and Variations

3 taps (1 measure) precede music

Theme

Marin Marais
(1656-1728)

Moderato

mf

p

Var. I

L'istesso tempo

p

20

3 taps (1 measure) precede music

Var.II
Allegretto

Var.III
Energico

3 taps (1 measure) precede music

3 taps (1 measure) precede music

The Secret

J.F.E. Gautier
(1822-1878)

4 taps (2 measures) precede music

Allegretto

Sonata Movements

from Six Sonatas for Violin

Willem de Fesch
(1687-1761)

8 taps (1 measure) precede music

Largo (in 8)

mf

meno f

4 taps (1 measure) precede music

Moderato

Allemande

mf

A

5 taps (1 2/3 meas.) precede music

Larghetto

Aria

4 taps (2 measures) precede music

Vivace

mf

Engraving: Wieslaw Novak

This is Alfred Lang's third recording for the Music Minus One Group. His two earlier recordings received favorable reviews in both the *International Trumpet Guild (ITG) Journal* and the *Brass Player Journal*. He has played solo E-flat cornet and toured extensively with both the Gold Rush Cornet Band and the New Custer Brass Band. A recording of "Custer's Last Band – The Original Music of Felix Vinatieri" is available through America's Shrine to Music Museum in Vermillion, South Dakota (www.usd.edu/smm).

Mr. Lang is an active freelance trumpeter in Southern California where he taught for twenty years at the University of Calfornia, Irvine and other campuses such as Concordia University and Saddleback College. His article on alternate fingerings was published by the *ITG Journal*; his reviews of recorded music have been featured in the *American Music* journal, published by the University of Illinois Press. He is a regular staff member at the Brass Chamber Music Workshop, which occurs each summer at Humboldt State University in Arcata, CA. Mr. Lang lives on the edge of the Cleveland National Forest with his wife and twin boys.

MORE GREAT BRASS PUBLICATIONS FROM
Music Minus One

CLASSICAL PUBLICATIONS

J.S. Bach –
Two-Part Inventions
& Other Masterworks for
Two Trumpets
Trumpet Edition
Performed by Robert Zottola
Book/Online Audio
00124386 .... $19.99

W.A. Mozart –
Horn Concertos
No. 2 in E-Flat Major, KV 417
No. 3 in E-Flat Major, KV 447
French Horn Edition
Performed by Willard Zirk
Accompaniment: Stuttgart
Festival Orchestra
Book/Online Audio
00400388 .... $19.99

Igor Stravinsky –
L'Histoire du Soldat
Performed by Gerald Kocher,
trumpet; Sean Mahoney,
trombone
Accompaniment: Parnassus
00400442 **Trumpet**....... $19.99
00400452 **Trombone**.... $19.99

Advanced
Trombone Solos
Accompaniment: Harriet
Wingreen, piano
Book/Online Audio
00400694 **Volume 1**..... $14.99
Book/CD Packs
00400149 **Volume 2** $14.99
00400738 **Volume 3** $14.99
00400739 **Volume 4** $14.99
Downloadable Edition
01007390 **Volume 5**....................... $14.99

Intermediate
French Horn Solos
Performed by the Jersey State
Jazz Ensemble
Downloadable Editions
01007043 **Volume 1**...... $14.99
01007325 **Volume 2**...... $14.99
01007327 **Volume 3**...... $14.99
Book/CD Pack
00400395 **Volume 4**...... $14.99

JAZZ/STANDARDS

20 Dixieland
Classics
Trumpet Edition
Performed by John Hoffman
Accompaniment: The Dixieland
All-Stars
Book/Online Audio
00400617 .... $14.99

Play the Music of
Burt Bacharach
Performed by the Jack Six
All-Star Orchestra
Book/Online Audio
00400647 **Trumpet**....... $14.99
Book/CD Pack
00400651 **Trombone**.... $14.99

Classic Ballads
for Trombone
Trombone Edition
Performed by Ira Nepus
Book/CD Pack
00131620 .... $14.99

From Dixie to Swing
No. 1 in D Major, No. 2
in A Minor, No. 3 in G Minor
Performed by Dick Wellstood
All-Stars
Book/Online Audio
00400619 **Trumpet**.......... $14.99
Book/CD Pack
00400622 **Trombone**....... $14.99

The Isle of Orleans
Performed by
Tim Laughlin's
New Orleans All-Stars
Book/2-CD Packs
00400446 **Trumpet**....... $14.99
00400461 **Trombone**.... $14.99
00400503 **Tuba** $14.99

New Orleans Classics
The Chicago & New
York Jazz Scene
Performed by Tim Laughlin's
New Orleans All-Stars
Book/2-CD Packs
00400025 **Trumpet**....... $19.99
00400026 **Trombone**.... $19.99

Music for Brass
Ensemble
Performed by Tim Laughlin's
New Orleans All-Stars
Book/CD Packs
00400432 **Trumpet**....... $14.99
00400451 **Trombone**.... $14.99
00400519 **Tuba** $14.99
Downloadable Edition
01007040 **French Horn**. $14.99

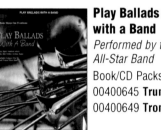

Play Ballads
with a Band
Performed by the Bob Wilber
All-Star Band
Book/CD Packs
00400645 **Trumpet**....... $14.99
00400649 **Trombone**.... $14.99

Signature Series
Trumpet Editions
Performed by Bob Zottola
Book/CD Packs
00138903 **Volume 1**..... $14.99
00142697 **Volume 2**..... $14.99
00147464 **Volume 3**..... $14.99

Swing with a Band
Performed by Steve
Patrick, trumpet; Roy
Agee, trombone
Book/CD Packs
00400646 **Trumpet**....... $14.99
00400650 **Trombone**.... $14.99

To see a full listing of
Music Minus One publications, visit
halleonard.com/MusicMinusOne

Music Minus One
HAL•LEONARD®
Prices, contents, and availability subject
to change without notice.